My Cookbook of
Baking

Laura and Jess Tilli

QED Publishing

Difficulty rating

⭐ Easy peasy!

⭐⭐ Pretty simple

⭐⭐⭐ Getting tricky

⭐⭐⭐⭐ Chef's challenge

⭐⭐⭐⭐⭐ Super chef!

Always ask for an adult's help when you see these symbols:

 An oven or hob is needed, or a hot item is handled.

 An electrical appliance, such as an electric whisk is needed.

 A sharp object, such as a knife or grater is needed.

Editor: Lauren Taylor
Designer: Andrew Crowson
Photography: Catrin Arwell

Copyright © QED Publishing 2012

First published in the UK in 2012 by
QED Publishing
A Quarto Group company
230 City Road
London EC1V 2TT

www.qed-publishing.co.uk

A catalogue record for this book is available from the British Library.

ISBN 978 1 84835 869 0

Printed in China

Serving sizes are approximations only.

All oven temperatures given are intended for fan assisted ovens.
Standard conversions are given below:

Electric (fan) °C	Electric (no fan) °C	Gas mark
90	110	$1/4$
100	120	$1/2$
120	140	1
130	150	2
140	160	3
160	180	4
170	190	5
180	200	6
200	220	7
210	230	8
220	240	9

Contents

Techniques

Rubbing

Put your flour into a bowl with cold butter. Using your thumbs and fingertips, rub the butter into the flour, lifting your hands up and down to get lots of air into the mixture. Keep rubbing until the flour and butter have combined into crumbs. Be careful not to over-rub as the mixture will become too sticky.

Pastry rolling

Sprinkle some flour over a clean work surface and your rolling pin. Place the chilled pastry on top. Gently roll your rolling pin backwards and forwards over the pastry, pressing down slightly, until it stretches. Turn the pastry around and roll in the other direction so the pastry stretches into an even shape. and thickness.

Cream whipping

Pour the cream into a large bowl. With a whisk, beat the cream as fast as you can until it thickens. Be careful not to over-whip your cream or it will curdle.

Tin greasing and lining

Rub a small amount of butter or oil all over the inside of your tin. Draw around your tin onto a sheet of greaseproof paper. Cut out the paper circle and place it inside your greased tin.

Egg separating

Carefully crack an egg over a bowl and catch the yolk in your hand whilst letting the white run through your fingers. Put the yolk into a separate bowl.

Egg beating

Using a fork, beat the egg until the yolk is completely mixed into the white.

Egg white whisking

Tip your whites into a large bowl and use an electric whisk to turn the whites into big white fluffy clouds. You can use a hand whisk too – it will just take a little longer, and more muscle power!

Folding

Very gently, move a metal spoon round the edge of your bowl then straight down the middle. Repeat until your ingredients are loosely combined. This technique is used to combine ingredients without stirring all the air and texture out of them.

Apple coring and dicing

Stand your apple up and carefully cut off each side until you are left with a square core to throw away. Chop the four sides you cut off into even cube-shaped chunks.

Icing piping

Place the nozzle on or inside the end of your piping bag. Roll the bag down until it is half the size. Spoon in your icing. Twist the bag closed and squeeze the icing right to the bottom and into the nozzle. Carefully squeeze your piping bag from the top to make the icing pattern.

Melting

Place your ingredients in a saucepan. Over a low heat, gently stir your ingredients together until melted and combined. Take off the heat before they start to sizzle or burn.

Cheese grating

With a large block of cheese in one hand and your grater in the other, move the block of cheese up and down over the grating holes, pressing quite firmly so that the cheese is shaved away. Don't try to grate very small pieces of cheese and because might hurt your fingers.

Jammy coconut Squares

Rating ⭐

Ingredients:

175g soft butter
175g caster sugar
2 free-range eggs, beaten
2 tablespoons natural yoghurt
175g self-raising flour
1/4 jar strawberry jam,
    stirred to loosen it
50g desiccated coconut

Equipment:

1 wooden spoon
1 mixing bowl
1 square cake tin, greased
   and lined
    1 table knife

Preparation time: 20 minutes

Cooking time: 25 minutes

Makes: 24

1. Preheat the oven to 170°C. With a wooden spoon, mix the butter and sugar together until creamy.

2. Add the eggs and yoghurt. Mix until combined.

3. Add the flour and mix again.

4. Pour the mixture into your lined cake tin. Smooth it out to the corners.

Perfect to take on a picnic!

Tilli tip
★ ★ ★
You can also halve the ingredients to make 12 if you like.

5. Bake for 25 minutes, until golden. Once out of the oven, leave to cool in the tin.

6. Spread the jam over the sponge. Sprinkle the coconut over the jam.

7. When the sponge is completely cool, lift it out of the tin using the greaseproof paper. Cut into squares.

Banana and chocolate cupcakes

Rating ⭐

Ingredients:
150g soft butter
150g caster sugar
2 free-range eggs
200g self-raising flour
50g cocoa
1 mashed banana
Small handful of banana chips,
    to decorate

For the icing:
75g soft butter
75g icing sugar, sieved
1 tablespoon cocoa

Equipment:
1 mixing bowl
1 whisk
1 wooden spoon
1 dessert spoon
1 teaspoon
1 muffin tray
12 muffin cases
1 wire rack
1 sieve
1 piping bag and nozzle

Preparation time: 25 minutes

Cooking time: 20 minutes

Makes: 12

1. Preheat the oven to 180°C. In your mixing bowl, mix together the soft butter and sugar until creamy. Add the eggs and whisk until smooth.

2. Using a wooden spoon, carefully mix the flour and cocoa into the egg mixture.

3. Fold in the mashed banana. Line your muffin tray with your muffin cases.

4. Using your dessert spoon and teaspoon, place two spoonfuls of mixture into each muffin case.

You could use fresh banana slices instead of dried chips.

5. Bake for 20 minutes, until firm to touch. Leave to cool in the tray for a few minutes before transferring them to a wire rack to cool completely.

6. To make the icing, mix all the icing ingredients together until smooth. Transfer the mixture into a piping bag.

7. Pipe the icing into swirly waves on top of each cupcake. Top with the banana chips.

Strawberry jam shortbread

Rating ⭐

Ingredients:
250g soft butter
60g icing sugar
1 teaspoon vanilla extract
190g plain flour
60g cornflour
½ jar good-quality
   strawberry jam

Equipment:
1 mixing bowl
1 wooden spoon
1 sieve
1 baking tray, greased and lined
1 wire rack

Preparation time: 20 minutes

Cooking time: 15 minutes

Makes: 12

1. Preheat the oven to 180°C. Mix together the butter, sugar and vanilla extract until creamy.

2. Sift the flour and cornflour into the butter mixture. Mix well until you have a smooth dough.

Tilli tip
★ ★ ★
If your dough feels too sticky, dust your hands with a little flour before rolling the balls.

You can use any flavour of jam you like!

3. Using your hands, roll the dough into 24 small balls. Space them out on your baking tray. Flatten each ball slightly with your fingers.

4. Bake for 12-15 minutes, until your shortbread is golden brown. Transfer the shortbread to a wire rack to cool completely.

5. Sandwich pairs of the shortbread together with the strawberry jam.

11

Popping-candy muffins

Rating ★ ★ ★

Ingredients:
150g soft butter
150g caster sugar
2 free-range eggs
225g self-raising flour
2 teaspoons vanilla extract
2 sachets popping candy, 1 for
    mixture, 1 for topping

For the icing:
175g icing sugar, sieved
175g soft butter
1 teaspoon vanilla extract

Equipment:
1 mixing bowl
1 wooden spoon
1 whisk
1 muffin tray
12 muffin cases
1 wire rack
1 teaspoon
1 dessert spoon
1 piping bag and nozzle

Preparation time: 25 minutes

Cooking time: 20 minutes

Makes: 12

1. Preheat the oven to 180°C. Mix together the butter and sugar using a wooden spoon.

2. Whisk the two eggs into the butter mixture. Stir in the flour, vanilla extract and one sachet of popping candy. Line your muffin tray with the muffin cases.

3. Using a teaspoon and dessert spoon, place a spoonful of mixture into each case.

4. Bake for 20 minutes, until the muffins are golden brown.

Try this!
★ ★ ★

Replace the popping candy with tiny sour sweets for tongue-tingling sour muffins!

The popping candy will really surprise your friends!

5. Leave the muffins in the tray to cool for a few minutes. Transfer to a wire rack to cool completely.

6. To make the icing, mix together the icing sugar and butter. Stir in the vanilla extract and transfer the mixture to a piping bag.

7. Pipe a small amount of icing on top of each muffin. Sprinkle with popping candy before the icing dries.

Sausage and apple pastry puffs

Rating ★ ★

Ingredients:

1 x 375g packet ready-rolled
     puff pastry
500g sausage meat
1 apple, finely chopped
1 medium onion, finely chopped
2 cloves garlic, crushed
1 egg, beaten
Salt and pepper
Ketchup, to dip

Equipment:

1 mixing bowl
1 wooden spoon
1 pastry brush
1 table knife
1 baking tray, greased and lined

Preparation time: 30 minutes

Cooking time: 25 minutes

Makes: 12

1. Preheat your oven to 180°C. Unroll the pastry onto a flat, clean surface.

2. In a large bowl, mix together the sausage meat, apple, onion, garlic and salt and pepper.

3. With your hands, scoop out the sausage mixture and place onto the pastry, making a long sausage shape down the middle.

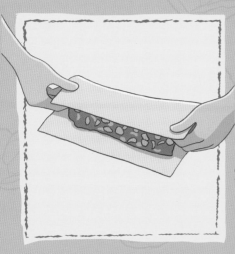

4. With a pastry brush or your fingers, brush the beaten egg down both sides of your pastry. Fold the pastry over the sausage meat and press down to firmly to seal.

5. Slice the sausage into 3 cm slices, and make a slit in the top of each one with a table knife.

6. Place the sausage rolls onto your lined baking tray. Brush each one with beaten egg. Bake for 25 minutes, until golden brown.

7. Leave to cool slightly before gobbling up, with ketchup to dip!

Try this!
★ ★ ★

Instead of apple, you could try adding rosemary and sage.

Dipping the puffs in mustard will be just as yummy!

15

Triple cheese muffins

Rating ★★

Ingredients:

100g soft butter
2 tablespoons olive oil
50g wholemeal breadcrumbs
3 free-range eggs
225g self-raising flour
1 teaspoon baking powder
75ml water
50g Cheddar cheese, grated
50g feta cheese, crumbled
Small handful of Parmesan
   cheese, grated
Small handful of pumpkin seeds
Salt and pepper

Equipment:

1 mixing bowl
1 wooden spoon
1 whisk
1 measuring jug
1 muffin tray
12 muffin cases
1 teaspoon
1 dessert spoon
1 wire rack

Preparation time: 20 minutes

Cooking time: 25 minutes

Makes: 12

1. Preheat the oven to 180°C In your bowl, mix together the butter, oil and breadcrumbs.

2. Whisk the eggs and a pinch of salt and pepper into the breadcrumb mixture.

3. Add the flour and baking powder to the bowl. Mix until smooth. Slowly stir in the water.

Seeds are a healthy snack!

4. Stir in the grated Cheddar and crumbled feta. Line your muffin tray with the cases.

5. Using the dessert spoon and teaspoon, carefully fill your muffin cases to about halfway. Sprinkle each with Parmesan cheese and pumpkin seeds. Bake for about 25 minutes, until the muffins have risen and are golden brown.

6. Leave to cool slightly in their tin, then transfer to a wire rack. They are delicious eaten while still warm!

Try this!

★ ★ ★

You can use any cheese you like – why not try crumbled Stilton?

Mini sausage-in-batter bites

Rating ⭐

Ingredients:

3 free-range eggs (cracked into a measuring jug)
Equal measure of plain flour to the eggs
Equal measure of milk to the eggs
24 small/cocktail sausages
12 teaspoons vegetable oil, plus extra for frying
Salt and pepper
Ketchup or mustard, to serve

Equipment:

1 mixing bowl
1 sieve
1 whisk
1 frying pan
1 x 12-hole muffin tray
1 teaspoon
1 small jug

Preparation time: 25 minutes

Cooking time: 20 minutes

Makes: 12

1. Preheat your oven to 200°C. Whisk together the eggs, flour, milk and salt and pepper, until you have a smooth batter. Strain the mixture through a sieve if you have any lumps.

2. Gently fry your sausages in a little vegetable oil until they are browned.

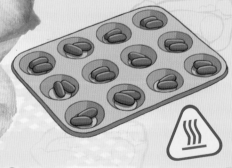

3. Place two sausages into each hole of your cake tray, with a teaspoon of oil in each hole. Heat in the oven for 5 minutes, until the oil is hot.

Perfect for party nibbles!

Tilli tip

★ ★ ★

It is important to heat the oil before adding the batter so it puffs up well and is crisp.

4. Carefully remove the tray from the oven. Using your jug, pour the batter into each hole, so that the sausages are slightly covered.

5. Return to the oven for about 12 minutes, until the batter has puffed up and is golden brown.

6. Serve warm with ketchup or mustard for dipping – or both!

Toffee apple layer cake

Rating ⭐

Ingredients:

175g soft butter
175g golden caster sugar
3 free-range eggs
175g self-raising flour
1 teaspoon baking powder
3 apples, peeled and diced
100g dark brown sugar
200ml double cream, whipped
Mini fudge or soft toffee pieces

Equipment:

1 mixing bowl
1 wooden spoon
2 spring-bottom cake tins,
  greased and lined
1 wire rack

Preparation time: 30 minutes

Cooking time: 25 minutes

Makes: 12

1. Preheat the oven to 180°C. Mix together the butter and caster sugar until creamy.

2. Mix the eggs, flour and baking powder into the butter mixture until you have a smooth mixture.

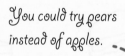
You could try pears instead of apples.

3. Divide the mixture between the two lined cake tins and scatter the diced apple over the top.

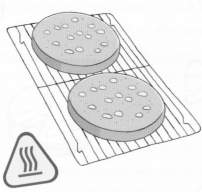

4. Sprinkle the mixture with the dark brown sugar. Bake for 35 minutes, until golden brown.

5. Leave the cakes to cool in their tins for 5 minutes. Turn out onto a wire rack to cool completely.

6. Gently fold your mini fudge or toffee pieces into the whipped cream. Sandwich your cakes together with the cream.

Try this!

★ ★ ★

You could replace the whipped cream filling with a thin layer of apple sauce for a lighter, fruitier taste.

Choc bread and butter pudding

Rating ★ ★

Ingredients:
8 slices of 2-day-old bread,
    buttered
1/2 jar chocolate spread
100g chocolate chips
100g sultanas
2 free-range eggs
250ml milk
2 tablespoons sugar
Custard, to serve (optional)

Equipment:
1 table knife
1 medium casserole dish or
    loaf tin, greased and lined
1 mixing bowl
1 whisk

Preparation time: 15 minutes

Cooking time: 40 minutes

Serves: 4–6

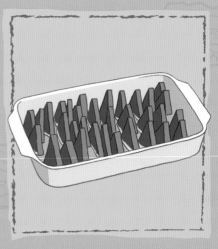

1. Preheat the oven to 180°C. Spread each slice of buttered bread with a generous layer of chocolate spread, and cut into four triangles.

2. Layer the triangles in your casserole dish with the points facing up.

3. Sprinkle over the chocolate chips and sultanas.

4. In a mixing bowl, whisk together the eggs and milk. Pour the egg mixture all over your chocolate bread.

5. Sprinkle over the sugar and bake for 40 minutes, until the egg mixture has set and the bread points are golden brown.

Try this!
★ ★ ★

You could add fresh banana slices between the bread layers too!

6. Cut into slices and serve with custard for a delicious treat!

Any kind of dried fruit will work well in this pudding.

Very berry crumble

Ingredients:

500g mixed berries, fresh
 or frozen
50g caster sugar
175g plain flour
100g soft butter
100g light soft brown sugar
50g porridge oats
Small handful of pumpkin seeds

Equipment:

1 saucepan
1 wooden spoon
1 mixing bowl
1 large ovenproof casserole dish

Preparation time: 30 minutes

Cooking time: 25 minutes

Makes: 12

1. Preheat the oven to 180°C. Gently heat the berries and caster sugar in a saucepan until slightly soft. If using fresh berries, add a little water to the pan. Place the mixture into the pie dish.

2. For the crumble topping, gently rub the flour and butter in a bowl, using your fingertips, until the mixture looks like breadcrumbs.

3. Carefully mix the brown sugar and oats into the crumble mixture.

Seeds give the topping a delicious crunch!

4. Sprinkle the crumble mixture over the berries. Scatter the pumpkin seeds over the crumble.

5. Bake for 30 minutes, until the crumble is golden and the berries are bubbling!

Tilli tip

⭐ ⭐ ⭐

Try serving this warm with custard or vanilla ice cream.

Raspberry and almond pan bake

Rating ★★

Ingredients:
3 tablespoons vegetable oil
3 free-range eggs (cracked into a measuring jug)
Equal measure of plain flour to the eggs
Equal measure of milk to the eggs
3 tablespoons caster sugar
150g raspberries
100g flaked almonds
Icing sugar, to dust
Custard or ice cream, to serve (optional)

Equipment:
1 ovenproof shallow dish
1 mixing bowl
1 whisk

Preparation time: 10 minutes

Cooking time: 30 minutes

Serves: 6

1. Preheat the oven to 180°C. Pour the oil into your ovenproof dish, and heat in the oven for 5 minutes.

2. In a bowl, whisk together your eggs, flour, milk and sugar.

3. Remove your dish from the oven, and transfer your mixture into the dish.

4. Scatter over the raspberries and almonds. Return to the oven for 25 minutes, until the pan bake is puffy and golden.

Almonds and raspberries taste wonderful together!

5. Dust with icing sugar and serve warm with custard or ice cream.

Tilli tip
★ ★ ★

Be extremely careful when tipping your mixture into the hot oil in step 3, as the oil may spit.

The best baked potatoes

Rating ★★

Ingredients:
4 large jacket potatoes
½ tin baked beans
2 spring onions, snipped into
    small pieces
120g Cheddar cheese, grated
50g soft butter
Salt and pepper

Equipment:
1 fork
2 mixing bowls
1 wooden spoon
1 table knife
1 dessert spoon
1 baking tray

Preparation time: 20 minutes

Cooking time: 30 minutes

Serves: 4–8

1. Preheat the oven to 200°C. Prick your potatoes with a fork and cook them in the microwave for about 9 minutes, until soft. Leave to cool.

2. Pour the baked beans into your mixing bowl. Add the spring onions, a pinch of salt and pepper, and half the grated cheese. Mix well.

3. Cut each potato in half and carefully scoop out most of the potato from the skin into a small bowl. Keep the skins to one side.

Tilli tip
★ ★ ★
The potatoes may need more or less time in the microwave, depending on how big they are.

Great for a delicious lunch!

4. Add the potato and butter to the bowl with your other ingredients. Mix well.

5. Using a spoon, fill the cooled potato skins with your cheesy bean and potato mixture. Place on a baking tray.

6. Sprinkle the rest of the grated cheese on top of the potatoes. Bake for 20 minutes, until golden brown.

Garlicky mushroom pasta bake

Rating ★ ★ ★

Ingredients:

2 tablespoons olive oil
1 small onion, finely chopped
2 cloves of garlic, finely chopped
150g mushrooms, washed and sliced
5g fresh parsley, chopped
200g pasta spirals
100g cream cheese
50g Cheddar cheese, grated
Salt and pepper

Equipment:

1 frying pan
1 wooden spoon
1 saucepan
1 colander
1 spoon
1 ovenproof dish

Preparation time: 20 minutes

Cooking time: 25 minutes

Serves: 4–6

1. Preheat the oven to 180°C. In your frying pan, gently heat the olive oil. Add the onion and cook gently for 5 minutes, until soft

2. Add the garlic and mushrooms. Cook for a further 6-8 minutes. Add the parsley and a pinch of salt and pepper. Turn off the heat.

3. In the saucepan, cook the pasta in boiling water for 5 minutes. Turn off the heat. Drain well and return the pasta to the saucepan. The pasta should still be a little hard at this stage.

4. Add the cream cheese to the cooked pasta. Stir well. Add the garlicky mushroom mixture.

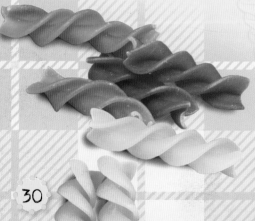

Try this!
★ ★ ★

Try using different types of cheeses for a different taste - how about Red Leicester or feta?

5. Transfer the pasta mixture into an ovenproof dish. Sprinkle with the cheese. Bake in the oven for 25 minutes, until the cheese is golden and bubbling.

Spinach and feta filo pie

Rating ★ ★ ★

Ingredients:

Olive oil, for frying and brushing
1 small onion, finely chopped
2 leeks, washed and chopped
250g baby spinach leaves
1 packet ready-rolled filo pastry
200g feta cheese
1 free-range egg, beaten
Small handful of poppyseeds
Salt and pepper

Equipment:

1 teaspoon
1 large saucepan with lid
1 wooden spoon
1 table knife
1 loose-bottom flan tin, greased
1 pastry brush
1 bowl

Preparation time: 30 minutes

Cooking time: 55mins

Serves: 6–8

1. Preheat the oven to 200°C. Add a teaspoon of olive oil to your saucepan and heat gently.

2. Add the chopped onions and leeks. Cook for about 10 minutes, until soft and slightly golden.

3. Add the spinach and a pinch of salt and pepper. Cover and turn off the heat.

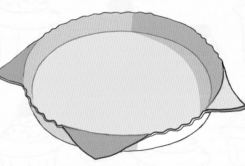

4. Unroll the filo pastry. Cut a strip off the top so that you have a square shape. Peel off one layer and place it on the greased flan tin, so it hangs over the edges of the tin. Brush evenly with olive oil, using your pastry brush.

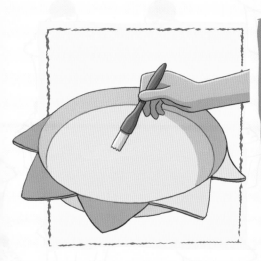

5. Peel off another layer of pastry. Place on top of the first layer, turning the tin so the layers form a star pattern. Brush with oil. Repeat with another three layers of pastry.

6. Crumble the feta cheese into a bowl. Add the onion mixture to the feta and mix well. Stir the egg into this cheesy onion mixture.

7. Pour the mixture into the pastry-lined tin. Fold the overhanging pastry into the middle. You may need to add a couple of extra scrunched-up sheets of pastry to fill any gaps.

8. Drizzle the pie with olive oil and sprinkle with poppyseeds. Bake for 45 minutes, until golden brown.

Tilli tip
★ ★ ★
You can use your fingertips to spread the oil instead of a pastry brush, but be careful not to tear the pastry!

Apricot jam tarts

Rating ★ ★

Ingredients:
100g plain flour, plus extra
    for dusting
100g cold butter
3 tablespoons water
1/2 jar good-quality apricot jam

Equipment:
1 mixing bowl
1 x 12-hole bun tray
1 metal spoon
Clingfilm
1 rolling pin
1 pastry cutter (slightly bigger
    than the bun tray holes)
1 teaspoon

Preparation time: 45 minutes

Cooking time: 25 minutes

Makes: 12

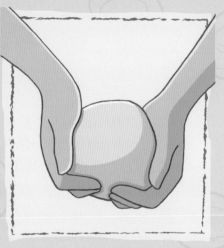

1. Preheat the oven to 180°C. Using your fingertips, rub the flour and butter together until it looks like breadcrumbs.

2. Fold in the water with a metal spoon, until the mixture comes together. Using your hands, shape the dough into a ball, cover with clingfilm and put in the refrigerator for 30 minutes.

Great for a summer picnic!

Tilli tip

★ ★ ★

You can use any flavour of jam for this recipe, or even marmalade or lemon curd!

3. With your rolling pin, roll out the pastry on a floured surface until it's ¼ cm thick.

4. Cut out 12 circles with your pastry cutter. Put the circles in the holes of your bun tray, squashing them down to the bottom.

5. Place a teaspoon of apricot jam into each pastry circle. Bake for 25 minutes, until the pastry is golden brown. The jam will be very hot, so wait for them to cool slightly before digging in!

Baked cheese with mini toasts

Rating ★★

Ingredients:

1 whole round soft cheese
    with rind (e.g. Camembert)
4 cherry tomatoes, halved
6 small sprigs fresh rosemary
1 small baguette
Olive oil
Sea salt

Equipment:

Baking tray, lined
Table knife
Chopping board
Bread knife

Preparation time: 10 minutes

Cooking time: 20 minutes

Serves: 12

1. Preheat the oven to 180°C. Place the cheese in the middle of the baking tray. Make 12 small slits in the top with your table knife.

2. Push half a cherry tomato and a sprig of rosemary into each slit.

3. Carefully cut your baguette into small slices. Arrange them around your cheese on the baking tray.

37

Try this!

If you don't like rosemary, you could swap it for small slices of garlic or some fresh basil.

This looks amazing on a buffet table!

4. Drizzle the bread with olive oil and sprinkle with a little sea salt. Bake for 20 minutes, until the cheese is melted and bubbling.

5. Cut into the top of the cheese and dip the toasts in.

Chocolate-anything biscuits

Rating ★ ★ ★

Ingredients:

80g soft butter
110g caster sugar
1 free-range egg, beaten
110g self-raising flour
100g of your favourite chocolate treat, such as chocolate raisins, chips or buttons

Equipment:

1 mixing bowl
1 wooden spoon
1 teaspoon
1 dessert spoon
1 baking tray, greased and lined
1 wire rack

Preparation time: 15 minutes

Cooking time: 15 minutes

Makes: 24

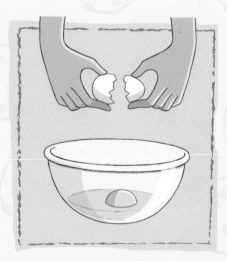

1. Preheat the oven to 180°C. Using a wooden spoon, mix the butter and sugar together until creamy.

2. Add the egg and stir well.

3. Add the flour and chocolate chips, raisins or buttons to the egg mixture. Mix well until you have a smooth mixture.

4. Using a teaspoon and a dessert spoon, place large spoonfuls of mixture 5 cm apart on your baking tray.

5. Bake for 15 minutes, until golden brown. Leave to cool on the tray for a few minutes,

6. Transfer your biscuits onto a wire rack to cool completely.

Add a mixture of white and milk chocolate for a yummy alternative!

Tilli tip
★ ★ ★
Don't put spoonfuls of mixture too close to each other on the baking tray or you'll end up with one big biscuit!

Peanut butter baked bananas

Rating ⭐

Ingredients:
4 ripe bananas
4 tablespoons peanut butter
1 small packet
    chocolate buttons
Icing sugar, to dust

Equipment:
1 table knife
1 tablespoon
aluminium foil
1 baking tray

Preparation time: 10 minutes

Cooking time: 30 minutes

Makes: 4

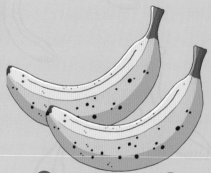

1. Preheat the oven to 180°C. Carefully make a split down the middle of each banana with a table knife. Be careful not to chop them in half.

2. Place a tablespoon of peanut butter inside each banana, smoothing it right down to the ends.

3. Place the chocolate buttons into the peanut butter. Wrap the bananas in aluminium foil.

You can use crunchy or smooth peanut butter.

👨‍🍳
Tilli tip
★ ★ ★
These work really well cooked on a barbeque for a summertime treat.

4. Place the bananas on a baking tray and bake for 30 minutes.

5. Leave to cool slightly, then unwrap. Dust with icing sugar and eat with a spoon.

Tray-bake pizza

Rating ★★★

Ingredients:

1 pack of ready-made
   puff pastry
Plain flour, for dusting
2 tablespoons tomato purée
½ tin chopped tomatoes
100g buffalo mozzarella
3 tablespoons green pesto
1 handful Cheddar
   cheese, grated
2 tablespoons olive oil
1 egg, beaten
Basil leaves, to garnish
Salt and pepper

Equipment:

1 rolling pin
1 baking tray
1 dessert spoon
1 teaspoon
1 pastry brush

Preparation time: 30 minutes

Cooking time: 15 minutes

Serves: 6–8

1. Preheat the oven to 180°C. Using a rolling pin, roll out the pastry on a surface dusted with flour into a rectangle slightly bigger than your baking tray.

2. Lay the pastry onto the tray. With your hands, fold in the sides to create a 1 cm border all the way round.

Try this!

★ ★ ★

You can add whatever toppings you like to this pizza. Why not try ham and sweetcorn?

Great to share
with friends at
a sleepover!

5. Brush all four edges of your pizza with the beaten egg. Drizzle with olive oil and sprinkle on a little salt and pepper. Bake for 15 minutes, until the pastry is golden brown. Scatter the basil leaves over the top before serving.

The olive oil will stop your pizza drying out while cooking.

3. With the back of a spoon, spread the tomato purée over the pastry. Repeat with the tinned tomatoes. Tear up the mozzarella into chunks and sprinkle over your pizza.

4. With a teaspoon, dot the pesto all over your pizza. Sprinkle over the grated cheese.

Twisty cheese straws

Rating ★ ★ ★

Ingredients:

1 x 375g packet ready-rolled
   puff pastry
4 tablespoons milk
50g Parmesan cheese, grated
50g Cheddar cheese, grated

Equipment:

1 pastry brush
1 table knife
1 baking tray, greased and lined
1 fish slice

Preparation time: 15 minutes

Cooking time: 20 minutes

Makes: 12

1. Preheat the oven to 180°C. Unroll the pastry onto a flat, clean surface.

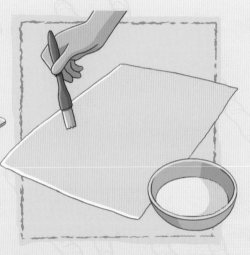

2. With a pastry brush or your fingers, brush the pastry with milk.

Tilli tip
★ ★ ★

After you've twisted your pastry fingers in step 4, squeeze the ends slightly to stop them unravelling.

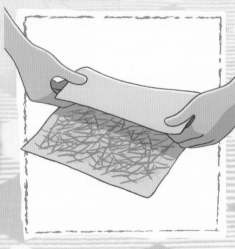

3. Sprinkle over both cheeses and fold the pastry in half. Slice the pastry into 12 fingers.

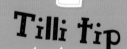

4. Carefully twist each pastry finger, then place onto your baking tray.

5. Brush the twists with more milk. Bake for 15–20 minutes, until the pastry is golden and the cheese is bubbling.

6. Leave to cool on the tray. Transfer to a serving dish using a fish slice.

Perfect for sharing with friends!

All-in-one breakfast bake

Rating ★ ★ ★

Ingredients:
1 tablespoon olive oil
2 sausages
2 rashers bacon
5 mushrooms, halved
½ tin tomatoes
2 free-range eggs
Chopped chives, to garnish
Buttered toast, to serve

Equipment:
1 frying pan
1 shallow ovenproof dish
1 wooden spoon

Preparation time: 15 minutes

Cooking time: 20 minutes

Serves: 2

1. Preheat the oven to 180°C. Heat the oil in your frying pan and gently sizzle the sausages and bacon until slightly browned. Add the mushrooms for the final 2 minutes of cooking time.

2. Transfer the sausages and mushrooms into your casserole dish. Pour over the tomatoes. Make two hollows in the mixture with a spoon and break an egg into each hollow.

3. Bake for 20 minutes, until the eggs are cooked through.

4. Sprinkle with chives. Serve with hot buttered toast.

Perfect for a lazy weekend breakfast!

Try this!
★ ★ ★
Use vegetarian sausages and bacon for a veggie version. Check the cooking instructions first.

47

Cheesy baked tomatoes

Rating ★★

Ingredients:

6 large tomatoes
100g firm mozzarella, grated
1 green pepper, chopped into
    small chunks
1 small tin sweetcorn
50g fresh parsley, chopped
2 tablespoons olive oil, plus
    extra to drizzle
Salt and pepper

Equipment:

1 sharp knife
1 teaspoon
1 mixing bowl
1 wooden spoon
1 baking tray, lined

Preparation time: 15 minutes

Cooking time: 20 minutes

Serves: 6

1. Preheat the oven to 200°C. Carefully slice the top off each tomato and place the tops to one side.

2. Using your teaspoon, scoop out the insides of the tomatoes and discard.

3. In your mixing bowl, add the cheese, chopped pepper, sweetcorn, parsley, olive oil and a pinch of salt and pepper. Stir well.

4. Using your teaspoon, fill the tomatoes with the mixture. Place the tomatoes on the baking tray and replace their tops.

5. Drizzle with olive oil and bake for 20 minutes, until soft and smelling delicious!

You can stuff the tomatoes with any vegetables you like!

Tilli tip
★ ★ ★

Beefsteak tomatoes are the biggest and are perfect for this recipe.

Raisin and cinnamon cookies

Rating ★★

Ingredients:
80g soft butter
110g caster sugar
1 free-range egg, beaten
110g self-raising flour
100g porridge oats
100g raisins
1 teaspoon cinnamon

Equipment:
1 mixing bowl
1 wooden spoon
1 dessert spoon
1 teaspoon
1 baking tray, greased and lined
1 wire rack

Preparation time: 20 minutes

Cooking time: 15 minutes

Makes: 24

1. Preheat your oven to 180°C. Using a wooden spoon, mix your butter and sugar together until creamy.

2. Add the egg to the butter mixture and stir well.

3. Add the flour, oats, raisins and cinnamon. Mix well until you have a smooth mixture.

4. Using a dessert spoon and teaspoon, place big spoonfuls of mixture 5 cm apart on your baking tray.

Try this!

★ ★ ★

Add half a teaspoon of ground ginger for a really warming flavour!

5. Bake for 12–15 minutes, until your cookies are golden brown. Leave to cool on the tray for a few minutes.

6. Transfer the cookies to a wire rack to cool.

Oats are a really healthy addition to cookies.

Knobbly-bobbly Shortbread

Rating ★★

Ingredients:

125g cold butter
55g caster sugar
1 teaspoon vanilla extract
180g plain flour, plus extra to dust
50g chocolate chips
50g glacè cherries, chopped
Handful of pumpkin seeds
Icing sugar, to dust
Sprinkles, to decorate

Equipment:

1 mixing bowl
1 wooden spoon
1 rolling pin
1 baking tray, greased and lined
1 table knife
1 wire rack

Preparation time: 50 minutes

Cooking time: 20 minutes

Makes: 24

1. Preheat the oven to 180°C. Mix the butter, sugar and vanilla together until creamy.

2. Stir in the flour until your mixture is smooth and forms a dough.

3. Add the chocolate chips, cherries and seeds. Mix well.

These are full of interesting textures!

4. Turn the dough out onto a clean, floured work surface and gently roll out until it's 1 cm thick.

5. Cut the dough into chunky fingers. Place them onto a baking tray. Dust with icing sugar and put the tray in the refrigerator for 30 minutes.

6. Bake for 15-20 minutes, until the fingers are lightly golden. Scatter with sprinkles, Transfer onto a wire rack to cool.

Tilli tip

★ ★ ★

Add the sprinkles as soon as the shortbread leaves the oven – they will stick in the soft dough.

Giant glitter meringues

Rating ★ ★ ★

Ingredients:
4 large free-range egg whites
200g caster sugar
Natural red food colouring
Fine edible glitter, to sprinkle

Equipment:
1 electric whisk or food mixer
1 extra-clean mixing
   bowl (not plastic)
1 metal spoon
2 dessert spoons
1 baking tray, greased and lined

Preparation time: 4+ hours

Cooking time: 30 minutes

Serves: 8

1. Preheat the oven to 150°C. Begin to whisk the egg whites in your mixing bowl with your electric whisk or in your food mixer.

2. Slowly add the caster sugar, a spoonful at a time. Keep whisking until the whites form a stiff mixture with no runny whites at the bottom of the bowl. Be careful not to over-whisk.

54

These will look fantastic at a glitzy party!

3. Add a couple of drops of your food colouring and swirl in gently with a metal spoon, creating a marbled effect. Be careful not to lose volume.

4. Using two spoons, place big dollops of the meringue mixture evenly over the lined baking tray, leaving space between each one.

5. Bake for 30 minutes. Turn off the oven and leave the meringues to dry in the oven for at least four hours, or preferably overnight. Sprinkle over the glitter to serve.

Really sticky flapjacks

Rating ★★

Ingredients:
100g soft butter
2 tablespoons golden syrup
100g soft brown sugar
250g oats
50g desiccated coconut

Equipment:
1 saucepan
1 wooden spoon
1 baking tray, greased and lined
1 table knife

Preparation time: 15 minutes

Cooking time: 25 minutes

Makes: 24

1. Preheat the oven to 180°C. In a saucepan, over a low heat, gently melt together the butter, syrup and sugar.

2. Turn off the heat. Add the oats and coconut. Mix well using your wooden spoon.

Classic flapjacks with a twist of coconut!

Tilli tip

If you dip your spoon in hot water before dipping in the syrup, it will be much easier to handle.

3. Pour the mixture onto the baking tray. Flatten out to the edges.

4. Bake for 25 minutes, until golden.

5. Using a table knife, carefully score the flapjacks into squares. Leave to cool in the tray before removing and dividing into portions.

Lemon and poppyseed bakes

Rating ★★

Ingredients:

200g soft butter
200g caster sugar, plus extra
    to sprinkle
3 free-range eggs
250g self-raising flour
2 teaspoons baking powder
Juice and zest of 1 lemon
2 tablespoons poppyseeds

Equipment:

1 mixing bowl
1 wooden spoon
1 square cake tin, greased
    and lined
1 skewer
1 wire rack
1 spoon
1 table knife

Preparation time: 15 minutes

Cooking time: 35 minutes

Makes: 24

1. Preheat the oven to 180°C. Using a wooden spoon, mix together the butter and sugar until creamy.

2. Add the eggs to the butter mixture. Mix well.

3. Stir in the flour, baking powder, lemon juice, lemon zest and poppyseeds. Pour the mixture into your cake tin and smooth to the edges.

4. Bake for 35 minutes, until a skewer inserted in the middle comes out clean.

5. Cool in the tin for 5 minutes. Transfer to a wire rack to cool completely. Sprinkle over a generous amount of caster sugar.

6. Slice into delicious squares before serving.

A light and refreshing snack for a summer's day!

Try this!
★ ★ ★
Try drizzling this cake with a little lemon-flavoured icing for an extra zingy finish!

Ham and Sweetcorn quiche

Rating ★★

Ingredients:

1 pack ready-rolled
    shortcrust pastry
½ onion, finely chopped
1 tablespoon olive oil
3 free-range eggs
4 slices ham, cut into
    small pieces
1 small tin sweetcorn
225g crème fraîche
75g Cheddar cheese, grated
Salt and pepper

Equipment:

1 loose-bottom flan tin
1 pair scissors
1 fork
1 frying pan
1 wooden spoon
1 mixing bowl
1 whisk

Preparation time: 30 minutes

Cooking time: 25 minutes

Serves: 8–10

1. Preheat the oven to 180°C. Unroll the pastry and lay it over your flan tin. Use scissors to cut the pastry to fit, leaving a 1-cm overhang all the way round. Press the pastry into the tin.

2. With a fork, prick holes all over the pastry and bake for 20 minutes. The pastry shouldn't turn golden yet.

3. In a frying pan, gently fry the onion in the olive oil over a low heat, until soft. Leave to cool.

4. In a bowl, whisk together the eggs with a pinch of salt and pepper. Stir in the ham, sweetcorn, onions and crème fraîche. Pour into the pastry case.

Tilli tip
★ ★ ★

This quiche is delicious cold. Why not wrap slices up in greaseproof paper for a picnic in the park?

Serve with a salad for a delicious lunch.

5. Sprinkle your quiche with the grated cheese and bake for 25 minutes, until the cheese is bubbling and the pastry is golden.

Mini cheese and ham toasty bakes

Ingredients:

12 slices brown bread
Butter, to spread
6 slices ham
100g Cheddar cheese, grated
Tomato ketchup, to spread
2 free-range eggs, beaten

Equipment:

1 table knife
1 small, round cookie cutter
1 baking tray, lined and greased
1 small bowl

Preparation time: 20 minutes

Cooking time: 20 minutes

Makes: 12

1. Preheat the oven to 180°C. Spread a thin layer of butter onto each slice of bread.

2. On six of the slices, place a slice of ham and a small handful of grated cheese.

Leave out the ham for a vegetarian version.

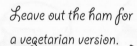

3. On the remaining 6 slices, spread a small amount of tomato ketchup. Make into 6 sandwiches with the cheesy ham slices.

4. Using your cookie cutter, cut out two circles from each sandwich.

5. Dip each circle into the beaten egg and place on the baking tray.

6. Bake the mini sandwiches for 20 minutes, until crisp. These can be enjoyed hot or cold.

Index